MW01248698

CLOSED

UNTIL FURTHER

NOTICE

# WHAT IS A PANDEMIC?

Heather C. Hudak

www.av2books.com

## Step 1
Go to **www.av2books.com**

## Step 2
Enter this unique code

**TORBK59DB**

## Step 3
Explore your interactive eBook!

**AV2 is optimized for use on any device**

# Your interactive eBook comes with...

**Contents**
Browse a live contents page to easily navigate through resources

**Audio**
Listen to sections of the book read aloud

**Videos**
Watch informative video clips

**Weblinks**
Gain additional information for research

**Try This!**
Complete activities and hands-on experiments

**Key Words**
Study vocabulary, and complete a matching word activity

**Quizzes**
Test your knowledge

**Slideshows**
View images and captions

## ... and much, much more!

Vi... ks.com

# WHAT IS A PANDEMIC?

## CONTENTS

# Pig Pandemic

In 2009, two children in California became sick with a new type of flu virus. They did not know each other. They lived 130 miles (209 kilometers) apart. Scientists called the new virus 2009 H1N1, or swine flu. They discovered that the virus passed to humans through contact with **infected** pigs. It could then spread from person to person.

Soon, people in Mexico and Texas had the virus as well. It was spreading fast. People all over the world began to get sick with H1N1. The World Health Organization (WHO) declared H1N1 a pandemic on June 11, 2009. Governments needed to find a way to stop its spread. People were told to avoid contact with each other. Some schools closed. Scientists worked hard to make a **vaccine**. It was ready to use by October. The vaccine stopped people from getting the virus. Finally, the WHO declared an end to the pandemic in August 2010.

The first case of H1N1 was discovered in San Diego, California, on April 15, 2009.

**FAST FACT**

During the pandemic, H1N1 infected about 61 million people in the United States. About 12,500 of these people died.

# Out of Control

**P**andemic is the word used to describe a disease that spreads around the world. The disease must affect a large number of people to be called a pandemic. It must put millions of people at risk. In most cases, a pandemic is caused by a new disease. People have not yet built an **immunity** to it. There is no treatment or vaccine for it. Not much is known about how the disease spreads or how to stop it. As a result, it spreads quickly and uncontrollably.

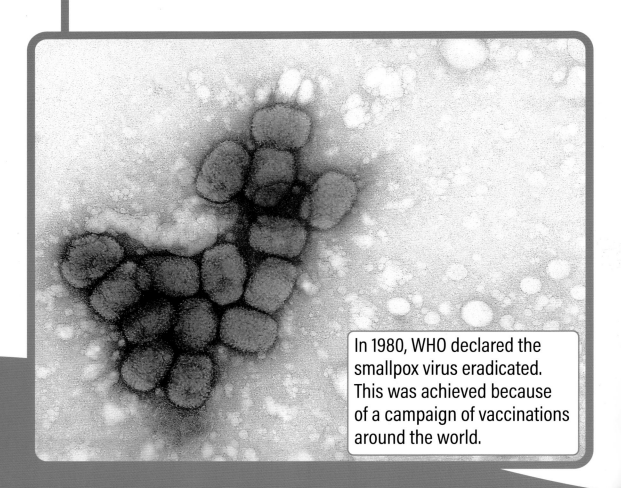

In 1980, WHO declared the smallpox virus eradicated. This was achieved because of a campaign of vaccinations around the world.

Diseases that are passed to people by animals are called zoonoses.

Most diseases that cause pandemics come from animals. People get the disease through contact with an infected animal. Often, the virus that causes the disease does not cause the animal harm. However, it may make people very sick.

## Outbreak, Epidemic, or Pandemic?

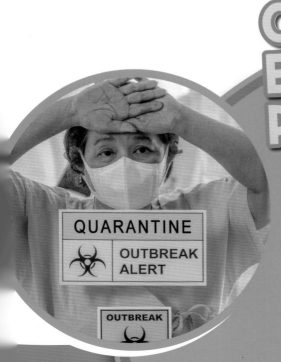

QUARANTINE

OUTBREAK ALERT

OUTBREAK

An outbreak happens when a disease spreads in a specific place over a certain amount of time. An outbreak with a sudden increase in cases over a larger area is called an epidemic. A pandemic develops when a disease spreads across a country, continent, or around the world.

# Countries Unite

No one knows when a pandemic might strike. It is important for countries around the world to work together when they do. The WHO is part of the **United Nations**. The WHO is the world leader on all health matters. This organization decides if a virus is a pandemic. The WHO also helps countries plan and prepare for pandemics. It sets standards that countries can use as a guide. The top **priority** for all countries is to stop the spread of the virus as fast as they can. The national government most often leads each country's pandemic plan. Local governments may decide what is best for their own communities.

Health workers also play a big role in pandemic plans. They help inform governments about the number of people who are sick. They also come up with ways to help stop the spread of viruses. Health workers must be ready to treat the sick as needed. They must also take care to protect themselves from viruses.

The Centers for Disease Control and Prevention (CDC) is the national health protection agency of the United States.

# WHO Regions

Countries that are part of the WHO are grouped into six regions. This helps the WHO work at preventing and controlling the spread of diseases.

Arctic Ocean

Pacific Ocean

Atlantic Ocean

Pacific Ocean

Indian Ocean

Southern Ocean

**LEGEND**
- African Region
- Region of the Americas
- South-East Asia Region
- European Region
- Western Pacific Region
- Eastern Mediterranean Region

SCALE
2,000 Kilometers
0    1,000 Miles

World Health Organization

The WHO was founded on April 7, 1948. Its headquarters are in Geneva, Switzerland.

# Get Ready

There may be big changes to daily life during a pandemic. People may need to stay away from each other to help stop the spread of the virus. Governments may stop travel between countries. Schools and offices may close. People may lose their jobs or become sick. They may not have enough money to pay for food or shelter. It might be hard for stores to get supplies or stay open. Factories might be forced to close.

Leaders of countries often worry about how they will help everyone. They may not have enough money or health supplies. Governments and health workers can offer guidance. People, family, and communities need to do their part, too. Communities can help by canceling big events. They may close parks and other spaces where people gather. It is important for people to obey rules during a pandemic. They are meant to keep people safe and well.

Wearing masks and practicing social distancing are often recommended during a pandemic.

# Roles and Responsibilities

This graphic shows the roles and **responsibilities** of people during a pandemic.

## Governments

Under the guidance of health professionals, they take decisions at a national or local level to keep people safe and limit the spread of a disease.

## Health Professionals

They have the scientific knowledge required to face a pandemic. They help people understand which measures should be adopted when fighting a disease.

## Individuals, Families, Communities, and Businesses

They listen to health professionals and government officials. They should follow the rules outlined by medical experts and authorities to help contain a pandemic.

# Stay Calm

It is important to stay calm during a pandemic. People often make poor choices when they panic. They may put themselves and others at risk. It is normal to feel scared, sad, or lonely. It can help to remember that others feel the same way and that it is okay to have these feelings. Being away from friends and family can be hard. Talking to loved ones using the phone or internet can help ease the mind. It is also a great way to make sure friends and family are safe and well.

Video-calling softwares can help people stay connected while they isolate during a pandemic.

Hobbies, such as painting or knitting, are great ways to pass the time and feel less worried during a pandemic.

Having a routine helps make life feel as normal as possible. Keeping the same bedtime and mealtimes is a good place to start. Teachers can send schoolwork for students to do at home. Reading books and watching videos are also great ways to learn. Adults can set up a home office to catch up on work. People can dance around the house, go for walks, or play sports in their yard to get exercise.

# COVID-19 and Mental Health

This graph shows the impact of **stress** on mental health in the United States during the COVID-19 pandemic.

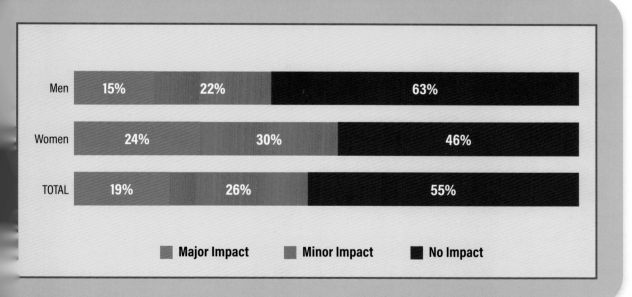

| | Major Impact | Minor Impact | No Impact |
|---|---|---|---|
| Men | 15% | 22% | 63% |
| Women | 24% | 30% | 46% |
| TOTAL | 19% | 26% | 55% |

# Learn the Facts

Scientists may not know much about a virus at first. Facts often change as they learn more. New details may be discovered daily. What may have been considered true in the past may not be true today. People need to keep up to date on the latest news. They need to know how to stay safe. Getting informed helps people make good choices.

The best way to get informed is to listen to what experts have to say. The WHO and the CDC give updates on pandemics. They post facts on their websites. Local health organizations also provide details on how to stay safe in their communities. People should always take the advice of doctors and other health experts. Doctors and health experts suggest which rules could be put in place to maintain the safety of all people.

It can take up to 15 years of study at the university level to become a doctor in the United States.

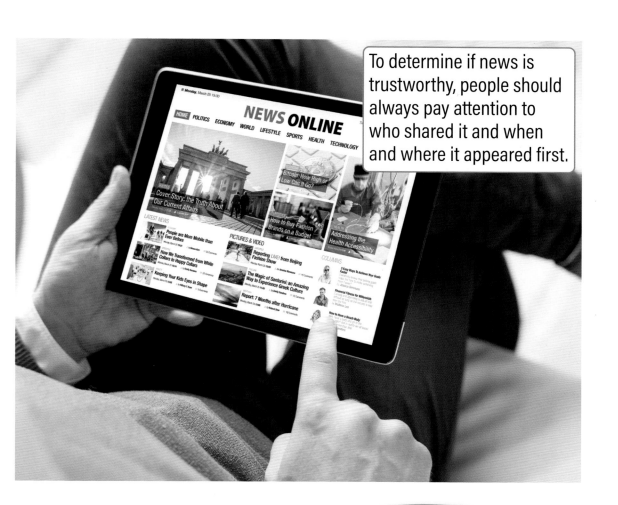

To determine if news is trustworthy, people should always pay attention to who shared it and when and where it appeared first.

# Trustworthy Sources

Some people post their thoughts and **opinions** on **social media.** Others talk about their ideas with friends and family. Not all the information they share is true. People should always check the facts with a trustworthy source. Sharing false information can be dangerous. People may not take the proper steps to stay safe if they do not receive the correct information.

# Know the Signs

It can be hard to tell if someone has a virus. Most virus **symptoms** start to show up a few days after a person is infected. The virus can spread before a person ever feels sick. Some people do not have any symptoms at all. However, they can still pass the virus on to others. Knowing how to spot the signs of a virus can help people stay safe in a pandemic. For example, coughing, runny noses, sore throats, and fevers are common symptoms of flu viruses.

People should not go to a hospital right away if they show any signs of a virus. They may risk spreading the virus to others if they leave their home. They should call their doctor to find out what to do. In most cases, virus symptoms are mild. People get better on their own. They just need to stay away from others while they are sick. In some cases, people need urgent care to treat a virus. A doctor will make plans for them to get the help they need.

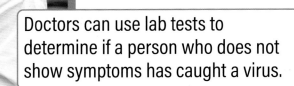

Doctors can use lab tests to determine if a person who does not show symptoms has caught a virus.

Understanding Viruses

# Prevent the Spread

There are steps people can take to help stop the spread of a virus.

**STEP 1**

Stay home from work or school.

**STEP 2**

Wash hands often with soap and water.

**STEP 3**

Cough and sneeze into a tissue or the bend of the arm.

**STEP 4**

Avoid close contact with others, especially in large crowds.

**STEP 5**

Get vaccinated.

**STEP 6**

Avoid touching the face, especially the nose, eyes, and mouth.

**STEP 7**

**Sanitize** objects and surfaces to kill germs.

**STEP 8**

Practice healthy habits, such as eating well, exercising, and getting plenty of rest.

# Past Pandemics

Pandemics do not happen often. These are some of the most deadly pandemics in history.

### Black Death
The plague pandemic known as the Black Death arrives in Europe. Historians believe the disease might have killed up to 60 percent of Europe's population.

**541–542**    **1347–1351**    **1889–1890**    **1918**

### Spanish Flu
The Spanish flu virus makes about 500 million people sick around the world. More than 50 million die.

### Plague of Justinian
Plague, a disease caused by **bacteria,** leads to one of the worst pandemics in history. It kills 25 to 50 million people in southern Europe, northern Africa, and eastern Asia.

### Russian Flu
In November, an outbreak of flu spreads in St. Petersburg, Russia. From there, the virus moves to the rest of Europe and the United States, killing about 1 million people worldwide.

## H3N2 Virus
A flu virus related to the H2N2 virus spreads around the world. More than 1 million people die.

## H2N2 Virus
A new virus kills about 116,000 people in the United States and 1.1 million people worldwide.

## 1957–1958  1968  2009  2019–2020

## H1N1 Virus
After starting in the United States, the H1N1 virus outbreak spreads around the world. Scientists believe the virus might have killed as many as 575,400 people worldwide.

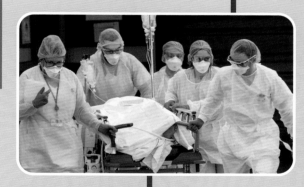

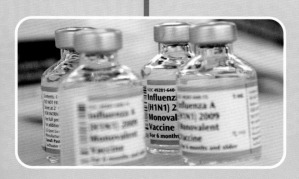

## COVID-19
The COVID-19 epidemic is officially declared a pandemic on March 11, 2020. The death toll keeps rising as the disease continues to spread.

# Plan Ahead

Pandemics are not sudden events. In most cases, people get a warning before a pandemic happens. There are things they can do to get ready. Planning ahead makes it easier to adjust when a pandemic does take place. A good first step is to make a list of emergency contacts. This might include doctors, family, teachers, and friends. Some people have health conditions that put them at greater risk if they get a virus. People should write down their health information in case they need help.

Stores may close during a pandemic. People could be stuck at home for a few weeks or even longer. They should make a list of supplies they might need. Pet supplies should be included on the list, too. It is important for people to buy only what they need. People should never **stockpile**. This helps make sure there are enough supplies for everyone who needs them.

It is good practice to prepare a pandemic kit that includes at least two weeks worth of food, water, and other supplies.

# Write a Public Service Announcement

A public service announcement (PSA) is a type of advertisement. A PSA provides information about an important issue. It is used to get people to take certain actions. A PSA may appear in a newspaper or on social media. It might run on TV or the radio. It can also be a poster or billboard. PSAs are often used during pandemics. They often provide facts about the virus. Some tell people how they can protect themselves and help stop the spread of the virus.

## Try writing your own PSA for a pandemic.

1. Use the internet to search for PSAs. Watch a few videos to get some ideas for your PSA.
2. Think about ideas for your PSA. Is there a problem you want to help solve? Is here an issue you want to tell people about? Make a list of all your ideas, and then choose one.
3. Come up with three questions you would like your PSA to answer. Then, research the answers.
4. Use a paper and pencil to draw a storyboard for your PSA. Think about what you want to show on screen. Then, sketch it. Include any words, images, or sounds.
5. Use a camera, a tablet, or a smartphone to shoot a video of your storyboard.
6. Share your video with classmates, your friends, and your family.

# PANDEMIC QUIZ

**1** When did the H1N1 pandemic start?

**2** What is a pandemic?

**3** Which group declares a pandemic?

**4** What can people do to learn at home during a pandemic?

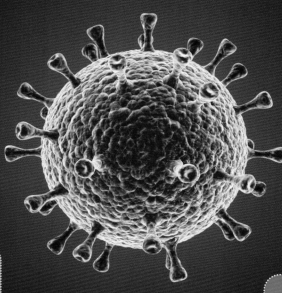

**5** What is the name of the national public health institute of the United States?

**6** Why is it important to stay calm during a pandemic?

**7** When was the WHO founded?

**8** Where can people find correct information about a pandemic?

# Key Words

**bacteria:** tiny organisms, each made of one cell

**immunity:** the ability to ward off infections

**infected:** came in contact with a virus that then entered the body

**opinions:** thoughts, beliefs, or points of view about someone or something that are not facts

**priority:** something that is very important and should be dealt with before other things that are less important

**responsibilities:** duties or tasks that a person is required or expected to do

**sanitize:** make something free from germs by cleaning it

**social media:** websites or applications where people share information and communicate with each other

**stockpile:** to keep a large supply on hand

**stress:** a feeling of being overwhelmed

**symptoms:** body changes that are consequences of a disease

**United Nations:** an organization that helps maintain world peace and gets countries to work together on common issues

**vaccine:** a substance made from a small amount of a disease that helps a person build immunity to it

# Index

# Get the best of both worlds.

AV2 bridges the gap between print and digital.

The expandable resources toolbar enables quick access to content including **videos**, **audio**, **activities**, **weblinks**, **slideshows**, **quizzes**, and **key words**.

**Animated videos** make static images come alive.

Resource icons on each page help readers to further **explore key concepts**.

Published by AV2
14 Penn Plaza, 9th Floor
New York, NY 10122
Website: www.av2books.com

Library of Congress Control Number: 2020941000

ISBN 978-1-7911-3250-7 (hardcover)
ISBN 978-1-7911-3251-4 (softcover)
ISBN 978-1-7911-3252-1 (multi-user eBook)
ISBN 978-1-7911-3253-8 (single-user eBook)

Printed in Guangzhou, China
1 2 3 4 5 6 7 8 9 0   24 23 22 21 20

072020
101119

Project Coordinator: Sara Cucini
Designer: Terry Paulhus

Every reasonable effort has been made to trace ownership and to obtain permission to reprint copyright material. The publisher would be pleased to have any errors or omissions brought to their attention so that they may be corrected in subsequent printings.

AV2 acknowledges Getty Images, Shutterstock, iStock, and Wikimedia Commons as its primary image suppliers for this title.